THE SILENCE OF HORSES

THE SILENCE OF HORSES

Lorne Dufour

CAITLIN PRESS

01 02 03 04 05 06 18 17 16 15 14 13

Caitlin Press Inc.
8100 Alderwood Road,
Halfmoon Bay, BC V0N 1Y1
www.caitlin-press.com

Edited by Peter Quartermain.
Text design by Kathleen Fraser.
Cover design by Vici Johnstone.
Cover photo *Montgomery in the Pines* by Molly Krimmer.
Printed in Canada.

Caitlin Press Inc. acknowledges financial support from the Government of Canada through the Canada Book Fund and the Canada Council for the Arts, and from the Province of British Columbia through the British Columbia Arts Council and the Book Publisher's Tax Credit.

Library and Archives Canada Cataloguing in Publication

Dufour, Lorne, 1940-
     The silence of horses / Lorne Dufour.

ISBN 978-1-927575-09-3

     I. Title.

PS8557.U2966S55 2013   C811'.54   C2013-902203-1

I dedicate this book to Diana, my wife, who not only knows all my poems, but has inspired this family almost forty years now.

I am forever grateful to my editor, Peter Quartermain. He is a great teacher who has helped me to see more clearly. I am also grateful to our publisher, Vici Johnstone. Vici, thank you for your patience.

CONTENTS

ONE

Horseshoe Nail

Such a fine piece
of industrial development

shaped to enter the safe side
and exit the safe side

a pure kind of steel
with something like lead

mixed into it
allowing a type of softness

which retains the ability to hold
and to bend without breaking

long and tapered so perfectly
one of the most beautiful

ever and forever connecting pieces
between us the people

and them the great horses
hallelujah for horseshoe nails

Anahim Lake Visit

When the children went into the school
he came to us, visiting for a few hours
appeared at the trailer with a large bullet hole
right through his back leg
he showed it to all of us
we fed him, made friends
deciding to take him to the vet's
next day in Williams Lake

he loved all of us
Sheba the collie too,
you could see their happiness
sharing the yard as a dog's kingdom
and he was assuming the appearance
of a royal Siberian Husky

left him with Sheba for a while
and when we returned everything:
the air, our expectations,
the importance of our gathering,
everything was filled with his absence

we spent the entire morning searching
drove every street and road
both on the reserve and throughout
the non native area,
children remembered him
but no one ever saw him again

my son said we were wasting time
because he was not just a Siberian Husky
he sadly explained, we won't find him,
he found us, he is a spirit dog

Gesture

With woman it's different
like the time we visited
Fish Lake the Fish Lake
where the school functioned

perhaps it was the acid
perhaps not but the chickens
they kept running in terror
in their roofless coop
staring up into the sky
filled with promises
only chickens understand

a large eagle was perched
high in a giant fir
that was it, why they knew
the real terror of possibility

I remember shouting at the eagle
calling it a chicken-shit hunter
go find something wild and free
I told him like a dream maybe
leave the chickens alone
you coward I shouted

the eagle knew me
he just laughed his screechy laugh
I could hear him across the lake
and so could the chickens

Our Lake

A mere glance
first thing this morning
engenders a deep peacefulness
we were never told to share

perhaps because our reason
for existence is water itself
no more no less

perhaps a deep loon loneliness
stirs inside of us lost memories
we can never afford to lose

great visitors come spring
the giant swans touch us
with their grace
flocks of geese
transform thunder
into song

the lake itself reflects
on certain days at certain times
reflects something more than the place,
the forest and the sky overhead
something inside

perhaps itself

My Best Friend

The rifle barrel still hot
and except for the flash of blood
on his deep chest the dog lay as if asleep
and I sat for a moment on the veranda
the gun across my knees,
my dog the puppy
I had once held in my arms
as one would a baby
he had bonded with me so fast
even following me to work
miles into the woods
sniffing out my trail
through deep snow
and I would find him
curled up by my fire
waiting all day
to come home with me

now as we cross to this
this darkness, this terrible place
my small son, nine years old
stooping to kiss the dog's head
and the dog suddenly snarling,
ripping inch-long fangs
into his face
tearing the cheek muscles
like scissoring through cloth,

puncturing the neck
missing the jugular
by less than a son's
finger nail

tearing the small face
into a mass of blood and terror
but most of all sadness
first trust betrayed
so young to learn
life's lesson
he put his little arm
round my neck and said
come to the hospital
with me Dad, please
come with me
and there was blood
on my neck where his arm
had circled it

The Turtle

My brother so gentle
small birds land on him
calling him father
while he lives
beyond ambition
telling me to come
and meet the turtle

way up high
on the mountain
and him climbing without boots
barefoot as if sky diving
till we greet the turtle

large stone turtle
shielded by the sky
an annual ceremony
each to place a single stone
until the turtle is so heavy
the mountain will sink
into the promises
of Lake Dubourn

needing rest we linger
protected by the inukshuk
we lay our old bodies out
Eskimo-elder style
watching clouds draw directly
overhead bringing faces, animals,
birds of passage, dragons,
images to suddenly disappear

the clouds came
from all directions
old friends, relatives
loved ones sudden and strong
gathering to speak to us
using speed and light
in the language
of a stone turtle

Miss Kenny

We inherited her thinking
she was a he till
we got to know
so we added Miss
to her moniker

now she is growing old
sits near the window
meditating upon the airborne
chickadees, woodpeckers, big beakers
crowd around the feeder

I can almost read
her thoughts
switching her long tail
back and forth
side to side
long needle
of some strange clock

the tiny creatures
just tease her
flaunting cherished secrets

Surreal

New pavement
no lines marked yet
its blackness so constant
so clean and unblemished
it startled Mother Bear
and her two cubs

emerged from the forest
where darkness is part
of the shadow world
to find a long ribbon
of almost perfect after-rain
darkness out in the near blinding
sunlight it stopped Mother Bear
in her tracks
her cubs stood
beside her statuesque

some trucks and cars went by
still they stood
totally immobilized
a dream reality
so totally unexpected
winding in silence
through the forest
where they dwell

Foxy Lady

She arrived as if she had decided
to be built into words so that
everyone could meet her sooner
or later and in my case
later usually works
when we discover something worth sharing

using a tin of molasses
which I finger painted
onto the horse's bits
making the bridles
something to be enjoyed
rather than just another
bit of surrender
one morning that procedure
revealed her presence
when the opened molasses tin
simply disappeared

she began appearing
at lunch time very carefully
walking a line between tenderness
and terror she came punctuating
the offer to share lunch
if we would provide extras:
half of our sandwiches,
pieces of ripe cheese,
even fried potatoes
greased and coated
with bacon memory
naturally we agreed

her companion came as well
obviously a male fox
a little scraggly his coat
spiky looking
drawn up in the midriff
but wide eyes clear
as green stars

her legs not as long
not skinny and all black
much more shadings of light colors
brown running into desert red
where soil luffs up iron
coloured and solar brushed
pure white socks on her front feet
and delicate white markings
on her pretty face
her tail wider and thicker
deeper red white tipped

I could see them curled up
in winter their tails shielding
and the white tips blending them
into the snow
they all but disappear
she carried the tail as a flag
announcing the presence
of wild beauty
while us loggers slipped
into silence
such wild beauty
shared with us

Eagle Words

I sailed across the lake
wind took me there
I circled below the nest
greeting the baby eagle

he'd climb up
rimming the nest
pyramiding his wings
become a grey sculpture
gleeking and gerbing in response

anxious parents came
cautioning everyone
and then one windless day
the family was gone

no dead eagle
under the nest
the young eagle's life
had begun

this early spring
sighting an eagle
I canoed over walked
into the ancient circle
centred by the nest

eagles came screaming at me
one giant wing a foot wide
soared overhead
rumbling thunder down
through the green trees

his partner arrived
circling the nest
protecting a chick so high
in the sky telling me
eagle hope has survived

we humans counting
science prayers
carbon-parts-per-million
beg second chance remission
while eagles make
babies this spring
in promise

Snowflake

One very tiny snowflake
isolated itself on the side
of your red winter boot
such a gentle suggestion

as you lie on your side
armed with a hair-dryer
fighting invading ice
in our waterline
the snowflake
lifts you

it connects you
to the stars

TWO

A View

Briefly, gracefully
children swoop past on bicycles
their heads contoured by helmets
inverted Tritons
strange alien shapes
humans with the heads of fish

up the street vehicles gather
a school of dark fish
entering a deep-sea coral chamber
some carrying the black roses
of Kosovo suddenly penetrating
our thoughts with painful light

post brain surgery
intelligence   shipwrecked
in the sea   of sentiment
while images of refugees huddle
in plastic homes
sudden decadence
beyond even the street-people
scene

a small country transformed
from a pastoral dream
into an urban nightmare
viewed on TV by us
the viewers of humanity

arriving at last
where children gather
at some park
a modern dragon
firing power balls
at young knights
brandishing great swords

Under Prince's Belly

I sit sometimes
under my horse
to eat my lunch

I sit with my back
to a tree with my feet
stretched right under
his boat-like belly

he feasts
on alfalfa hay
and I drink my coffee
in the cool shade
of his body

I think of giants
because he is gigantic
my gentle, powerful friend

were he to step on my leg
the bones would be crushed
but he knows this
and as I watch him
so totally tuned in
to every sound, every
wind I think of what
this gentle giant
so surely knows

Winter Blues

Mid January in the Cariboo
rain falling like curse words
and us burning brush
gathered up with horses

snakey cloud of smoke
comes clinging to the ground
me and Tyler standing sort of
sculptured into winter misery
and the horses suddenly disappear
as if they were evolving
into myth

later, driving Old Granny
1956 D6 Cat, hoping
to help the horses
Granny blew herself
right off her own track
a misadventure involving me
with the sky's vocabulary

one of those cold days working with Tereina
our family princess and Chris and Tyler
young knights within her generation
and all of them soaked into their bones
not a freezing drop of the cloud curse
unworthy of this working man's poem

then heading home in darkness
climbing the hill where Granny broke down
our ancient Ford van, half dedicated
to pure rust and mobile atheism,

it coughed once just close enough
so despondent Granny could hear her
pulling the horse trailer
and then she died, mid stride

Chris off loaded the team
singling them out
rode home in proper style
with all of our machinery left behind
bad memories needing repair

Invisible Geese

A great flock
filled the sky
full of loneliness

it took a long time
before their cries
dwindled
dwindled down
into memory

so high they flew
I could not see them
yet I wondered
if they saw me
and wanted me
to hear them
sing their songs

Maison de Vieux

Within weeks the building rose
from a foundation of cemented love
it ascended into a multilayered structure
where hundreds of elders would reside
It was set up on a hillside
overlooking the sides of other buildings
and the wide lawns of city centre
and, of course, the traffic
of downtown adventurers

a most artistically built stairway
began winding its way up from
the sidewalk, built with stone slabs
making each step inexplicably important
and the stairs led into a flower-box
ending abruptly against the soil of the hill
leaving a hundred foot distance
to the doors of the retired

does the stone stairway
symbolize old age? Something
artistically suggested? Something
that stops abruptly before we get anywhere
or perhaps in a moment of charity
the stairway reminds the rest of us
who can still enjoy stairs that lead somewhere
to stay as far as possible away
from old age

Stove

Sad little stove
abandoned to endless solitude
without a house to heat
it stands out under aspen trees
winter once again covering
it with a clean white
blanket of snow

given as a gift
many years ago waiting
for something to fill
with its warmth and still
no floor under it no walls
no roof over it the beautiful
glass door reflecting darkness
hoping someday to be sparkling
this little brother
to the sun

it made its way back
into the woods it sat
for years and years
birds and bears visited it
squirrels recognized it
moose and deer included it
into their quiet surroundings
and humans walked past it so often
they began to forget it until
it achieved occasional invisibility
sometimes weeks slipped by before
anyone remembered seeing it
short and squat just like
this planet

Horse Freedom

Our horses immigrated
once again they have gone
to distant fields

government grazing official
warned us about grazing
upon Crown land

warned us that in this country
to go poo de gree
as the Romany say

that is a major sin
bypassing purgatory
taking us straight to hell

we told our horses
they know what the law
tells them they must do

but they do what they must
whenever they get the chance
and that's why we love them

Leonard

This legend of a horse
named Leonard
born so bright in black
and white, feathers
and a white brush stroke
down his beautiful black face
after twenty four years
surely he knows
soon he will die

we put him in the stocks
where we could hold him up
wide belt beneath him
we could inspect his legs
and his back feet
he has been limping

when I began to lift
his right back foot
he instantly collapsed
so we managed to place him
back on his four feet
applied antifungus
around his ankles where bumps
built up over the years

since he's been in the stocks
he trembles when he walks
his hind end is difficult
to negotiate
he is no great dancer now

tomorrow I will put him
into the barn and place something
across the door
so the other horses
won't bother him

nah I won't do that
he loves being with Montgomery
even if he doesn't seem to like
the new young team Lady and Jim

makes me realize
I must do a lot more training
so Lady and Jim will be loving
and gentle and generous
which is little to ask
compared to Leonard
they have light years
to travel as they become gentle
and easy to be with
whether it is eating together
or working with me pulling logs
or the sleigh and the wagon

Trimming Montgomery

Got his name birthing
Saint Patrick's Day
Montgomery after an Indian pal
a giant from the Stone Rez
now Monty pushing twenty five
years after many of our great ones
have gone ahead breaking trail
challenging he sets himself back
in the shoeing stocks
hating every single second
being held up by chains
much rather lean all twenty five
into solid trust for this meager
human frame when he could alter
my destiny simply straightening
out his leg larger than me
in total
placing me forever
on lunar real estate
but we insist, force him
into the stocks
an hour later
his hind feet look wonder sure again
reminding me of my love
telling me upon do-you-love-me-still?
and her saying well my feet
love your feet
while her toes rub my ankle
a naked moment in the stocks
both me and Monty
will never rejoinder

Full Moment

She sitting in my pick-up
asked if I believe
in something like a great pool
into which we poets
sometimes dip our pens

no, I said, I believe
as a busy chipmunk climbed
into the back of my truck

in light and sometimes
we find ourselves
full of the divine light
of existence
and sometimes we, as poets, discover
ourselves within such light

a small, twisted, golden leaf
spinning and spinning
on an almost invisible
silver thread it
had begun to fall
in the season
of its departure
a spinning dance

the sun
moved across
different green neighbourhoods

a beautiful whisky-jack
wisa-ked-jack
arrived gliding
sharing oats
with back-tethered horses

a natural symphony
of activity
while the leaf
in the breeze
still dervish

dancing

Gypsy Horses

They were my responsibility
Pride who was more beautiful than pride
and Chal the slightly over-tall Clydesdale
who had developed so much power
during his teenage years
a sort of blessed clumsiness
stayed with him
all his life

surely a graceful stumbler
mile after mile after mile
they pulled our stage-wagon
rolling through ripples
of the wind

with large wooden wheels
we trundled through the back door
of history making me wonder
would the jet age accept us
they might just think
we were a postcard vision
soon to be forgotten
though we knew
with Pride and Chal
we would always linger
in their dreams

magnificent Pride was an aristocrat
wherever he went people stared after him
children always insisted on petting
his long nose realizing that this magical horse
announced by the perfect balance

of his feathered hooves
they instantly returned
saw the bright tenderness
in his eyes

even for difficult humans
like myself it was impossible
not to love Pride as he walked
with such nobility alongside
stumbling Chal
while Chal's prolonged adolescence
always captured our hearts
stirring deep down
into our gentleness

The Silence of Horses

The rich countries
dedicated to capitalism
have developed quicksand
like income tax and deficit
types of logic
keeping the poor
in their proper accomodating places
while the rich peak out
on the pyramids

now as the systems fail
out of goodness we will stride
with our arms open
with the gifts of our technology
our medical knowledge and education
provided by reality

we need no longer hide
behind concepts of alienation
or the language of clever linguistics
while the poor are dying
we need the silence of our horses

Winter's Drum

Slowly the ice thickened
as the first deep freeze
swoops down from the arctic
this old half-deaf citizen
can hear the great rumbling
the drum booming cries
of the giant greeting
his own demise

having survived centuries
of insanity
we cling to the past
surely the comfort system
for the rich will work
once again
though deep drums begin
as the giant sheds
pyramid tears

the homeless prepare
for the hordes
and the lake echoes
our fear of the future

capital the giant
taller than the tower
in the bible
reaches into the darkest corners
of our hearts thundering
into oblivion

no longer
can we return
to give-unto-Caesar logic
knowing at last
that belongs to the past

Clydesdale Leonard

For Gabe and Venta

Born pure black with white socks
we called him Leonard after Cohen

now sometimes he tells me he wishes he was human
like how he fell in love with you that time

says you appeared wrapped up in a bath towel
long legs so beautiful and a smile

so promising somehow tied in with apples
and cob, oats and bran with corn pennies

crushed flat under a train of molasses
even though he is an elder now

he still feels that sometimes
as if he was a young stallion

a true Leonard Cohen with feathers
that keep him flying just thinking about you

whether he is floating down a skid trail
or out grazing with his sister Dora

going quietly across fields so wild
he forgets being old

Our Horse Dora

When I buried Dora
I placed an aspen cross
on her grave
I never heard of horses in heaven
and I plan to start a herd
I'll speak in sonnets
to get past St. Peter
and sweet Dora will greet me
as a beloved family member

I had promised her a stallion lover
but death came like a freight train
filled with volcanic steam
scattering all my promises
into the rain
I had hoped to leave first
and as a stallion
to return

my most intelligent friend:
even while leaving she trusted us
her body bloated up
her nostrils expanded
her heart and her lungs
strangled
any other creature
would have long since quit

but she kept getting back
on her feet
kept hope in us
a kind of grief

perfectly framed in the side mirror
of my old pick-up
suddenly she reappears
trotting home with us
her beauty demanding attention
making the green of grass more green
gentle ocean waves of golden rod
and roadside milkweed
tumbling mustard and sunflower, daisies
and blue clover
indian paint brush and endless clouds
of the wild pink rose and her
churning them into a mysterious
bagpipe symphony and all summer
we hear her music

The Wedding

For Troy and Ingrid

Wedlock is a wondrous ceremony
of clouds that we the children
of clouds celebrate in the skies
of our hearts

with buffalos, whales, dragons
unicorns and flocks of ships
full rigged with luminous sails
our loved ones often appear
their wispy smoke rings
float over sacred mountains

in wedlock we pledge our love
to the clouds, the curvaceous
buoyancy of tummy and breast
echoes the eternal acceptance
of how little we truly need
to know as our great ship
the Terra Firma holds fast
to its course through
the ever changing
transcript of windy
creation

Morning

Awaking together
having perked a cup
the perfect gift

celebrating last night
holiness of radical love
we begin the day sharing

one of Joe Blade's poems
as the moon and sun
create magical
recognition

two of our dogs
run upstairs and leap
into our bed nestling

then an aircraft
flies somberly over
startling the dogs
from their sleep

lifts them out of their
geological-time-clocks
shared with us

leaving momentarily
our bed to run and bark
at the airplane

while the human world
is in a big hurry
arriving somewhere
crammed full of
dog envy

Waiting for a Letter

It's kind of like the Cariboo hay
you might need it, your horse might
no more last year's

where is the sun
rain rain rain
we need a solid week
everything is ready
the timothy is desperate
I've noticed it waving
miniature Cuban cigars

I know that above the clouds
the sun is shining every day
it still exists, today today
it will break through the clouds
and bring its love to the fields
the blooming alfalfa
will sigh in relief
and all our horses
will survive another year
let winter come
let the letters come

Sleigh Ride

Finally snow has arrived
a deep powdery simplifier
which we all know
would wrap up the world

twenty below
fingers turning into ivory
like the keys of a piano
as the harness sorted
and dressed out

Kate the mare
and Star her young companion
and old Buddy our dog
barking his excitement
and me wearing bucking chaps
protecting my legs
in the wind

head out down the road
turning off half an hour
into the wild meadows
and the snow is so deep
the sleigh becomes a plow
pushing six inches
making Kate and Star
stumble and fall
they pull so hard

half a mile to home
becomes a Chilcotin journey
making demands extending the reins

so the front set of runners
begins to surf
still though we stop often
the horses not
in top shape

if more snow returns
Old Granny our D6 Cat
will have to work
but for now the trail
opens to perfection
and my sweetheart
all bundled
in her father's parka
with her cheeks rosy
winter flower
for the season

Lamplight

Full moon fills
eastern sky
pin point stars
silver sparks

darkness dismissed

mounted Dora
heading home

little man
riding home
near a mile

northern land
stillness
exists

my sweetheart
lit the lamp
set it centre

window
of the barn

Years Driving

Sickle moon a red sideways grin
a piece of petrified dinosaur bone
treasured by a family member
when life itself is tentative
left entirely to others
what they might say
or think or wonder

met me prepared
someone, like myself, heart attack
for three years returned to health
warning me after my two years
how his returned in vengeance
leaving him with no colour
with no strength
against gravity

we could taste the needles
in the coffee you made us
he confided that time
needles of pine
fir, spruce maybe
we both tasted them
your horses corralled
in the forest your
children tumbling
on the green
moose hide

Leader Mare

Four horses raised
away from rivers
or lakes whatsoever

as we neared
for the first time ever
the tiny lake I call my ocean

her nostrils flared
her ears began twisting
tuned to the silent music

when we arrived
the other three stood back
in total shock

while she walked
right into it
up to her belly

making large waves
crashing up on the shores
of this Mediterranean

she swung about
dancing a wide circle
returning belly deep

repeating her joyful
meeting with
her mother

she had never
visited a lake before
till she met

this lake in person
then while the others
just watched

she danced
the great dance
elephants understand

Francesca

An old pink shirt
a random bit of clothing
improvised into a sarong
already she has mastered
gypsy-style blossoming
her clothing sings
the song of freedom

already Franny is seven
more than a handfull
akin to magic eskimo
small Inuit bright eyed
so startling at times they flash
filling with star light deeper
and deeper when she laughs

I look closely into her eyes
when she is telling me something
absolutely important like:
hey Uncle are we going
for a sleigh ride?
I want to ride the GT snow racer
pulled behind the sleigh!

months ahead of the season
her imagination controlling time itself
already she is wearing her parka
winter boots and warm mittens
already she sees soft snow banks
steam puffing from the nostrils
of the giant horses
already she sees her uncle

as a winter shaman
already she is steering
her GT, everyone is laughing

her eyes and lips so expressive
come post puberty
she will transform frogs
into great warriors

THREE

Season of Wind

For Computer Lovers

A tall stand of spruce
across the lake
bends so dramatically
I wonder if the globe
has slipped a cog
somehow in the transmission
of the entire universe

mankind in its evolution
towards the singularity
of disease free
long life expectancy
having surpassed mythology
where once poor God
was not only accepted
but entirely loved
in old languages
now abandoned
in computers

ah but let us sing
the auld songs Chaucer sang
"wee Geoffray" setting someone up
for a gentle nudge towards love
hanging her lovely ass out the window
thinking the would be lover was confused
yet how he loved kissing her sweetly
every cubic centimetre of her loveliness
that won't ever fit properly
in a computer

Brady's Gift

A child's toy
simply a small plastic figure
mounted on helicopter wings
which turn when you pull a cord

winding the rider
into a fifteen-foot flight
straight up which veers
to the side
crashing without injury
each time

practicing little Brady steps back
trips over the concrete guide
in the parking lot

arms as big as wonder
and a small bruise appears
a tiny scratch achieving
constellation history

briefly I hold his elbow
diving all the horse power
ever felt through those bolts
of lightning called reins
and quickly he recovers

come to visit us soon
Mom asks him
yes but I won't bring
the three wheeler
says little Brady
because last time...
and he solemnly flips
his wrist to define
mankind's possibilities

Visiting Jerry LeBourdais

June 96

Found him top end of Horse Lake
old homestead, grey logs
white plaster and his fields
turned over like fresh blankets

his back to the wild country
as if he could still escape
meanwhile the G.C.D. (Great Condo Dream)
inching up the lake side, yeah
they're comin allright, he laughed
pointing down beyond the farm

young foreign couple visiting
dewy-eyed at the shrine of green
communing with the commune-man
living the powerful dream
gathering strength
to leave
     firm hands, clear eyes
let time and illness
falter his step, weaker
for sure but he walks
wherever he goes and
he believes even more
in the Cariboo potato

there's a field
on the way out, he said
all those dandelions
like the sun setting there

it's an organic farm too
(sparkle of pride in his eye)
watch for it Lornie

we seen it too
came round the corner
our giant horses shifting
in the big trailer
the field just like he promised
a mirror of gold
their iris of God's speckled eye
and earlier when little Easten
and Robin set their oranges
on the chopping block
to chase a chicken
from the shed
Gerry noticed the half-eaten orange
tumble into the dirt
Easten, he said, needs another orange!
like a royal proclamation
he fetched it, handed it to Easten
as we were leaving giving him
a brand new sun

Father Comes

Pushing 75, refusing to retire
he used to always say
when things go bad
they will likely
get worse

he'll visit soon
and down by Bear Creek here
broken fern, stinging nettle,
thistles, cooch grass, buttercup
gooseberry, everything crowding green

I stand here let my thoughts
grow into the total weed jungle
until tiny rootlets finger down from
my toes to anchor me here
reel me in this harbour of expectancy
and hold me strong

my father will understand
the clear mountain blood
of the creek, he will know
the endless hunger
of my soul and he will laugh
when I tell him how, after a while,
leaves, grey leaves, began to fall
from my hair when I was a tree

The Back Lane

I drove down the back lane
with all the houses
facing other streets
facing the future
on one side
facing the future
on the other side

I saw a giant
holding a small child
way up in the sky
the child could see
for a second
more than the giant sees
more than I could see

each lift
he was higher than before
flying through
the great blue sky
twisting
like Jet Man mid-air
he saw everything so clear
he could not let the giant
lower him to the floor

Fingers

That's what they call him
"Fingers" described as a gentle soul
by acquaintances and friends
who meet him as an equal

since my hair turned white
and stands up in all directions
sometimes the family calls me Fingers
last time I glanced at them
and began the little dance
Fingers always dances

most times when you see him
downtown in front of the mall
or the liquor store
he rarely moves more
than a foot or two
he does a little dance
with the cracks
of the sidewalk

knowing beyond doubt
and eventually beyond
everyone else's doubt
he is doing his part
to keep the planet
in perfect balance
with the universe

when you give him a buck
for a cup of coffee
or two for a donut and coffee

he just smiles slightly
says thank you
returns to his dance

when he looks at you
it is easy to see the gentleman
the sense of street royalty
he accepts kindness
as he should

Lake Mataninda Memory

Returned to the canoe
heading up Lake Mataninda
north of Penewibikong
"river-with-blind-arm"

great to be with you Dad
coming on the west shore
where the big dolmen
was left by the shaman

the wavy lake
rippled at the canvas
stretching like the light
across my sweetheart's cheek
true canvas over cedar frame

let the power of this place
enter our hearts
where the other shaman
erected that monolith
no one short of godpower
could have attempted

sort of eternal challenges
the two shamans outperforming
each other reminds me of Mom
and Dad heading up lake again
with the family just children

New Born

For Noah Geensen

How can I welcome you
with a story that so many
have already heard
one way or the other
but somehow I must
and let the rotund purpose
of my belly lead me on
beyond our simple pride as youth
achieved by some friend of mine
whose lovely woman told me once
she had accidentally discovered
a book of mine
filled, she said,
with many small poems
and still I forgave her
that beauty with her lover
in tow like a graceful barge
gently and slowly dancing
across the straight
where all lovers once rejoiced

now I let the belly toll
my honeymoon morning
still in song
after more than thirty
years as true as the sound
of our horses returning
like my poems promised
many years ago
yes little one

then with infinite graditude
your lips reach for the breast
memory will never forget
its largess retains this morning
magic for the moment
of your arrival
as the French proclaimed
forging through the wide
department store
discussing family as easily
as prices as they change

how can you love me still
she asks one mirror moment
as my body has grown so wide
large in its effulgence
motherhood will ever control
as I kiss so gently that tummy
and stroke with abandonment
the slope of her beauty floating
off with my love cloud
where forgiveness exists
far beyond necessity
While your mother
on that day of your arrival
filled with the elephant sized
freedom and pride of motherhood
itself another small poem part
of the story its moment unending
as an infinite number of expressions
reveal themselves before your face
becomes the living mask
you get to carry

towards your love cloud
there the very clouds are poems
the wind-twisting aspens are applauding
the musical symphony of geese
and the deep flute like echoing
of the ageless sandhill cranes,
the cottonwood buds reveal
an aroma we can all recognize
no matter how deeply
religion or philosophy attains
when we meet we are all
being born again

Arctic Curse

Twenty-five below this morning
two pair of felt-lined boots
huddle up to the wood stove
even though this winter
left us horse loggers
with real kleenex
on the table
rather than the usual
toilet paper compromise
March comes into spring
as an arctic curse

in the meantime
my sweetheart
informed me
that Bob Dylan's
singing backup
for Victoria's Secret
it's the angels he adores
the angels from Bhutan
all through the Himalayas
only born again into American flesh
all stirred up by freedom
and Dylan's adoration

Inebriation

Four too many
heading home somehow
the motion warns me
we must drive slowly
yet she drives in low gear
and still that speed
is killing me

turn around my dear
drive home in reverse
then motion too
will be reversed

once we find reverse
let's stick to that
until the world slows down
let's celebrate horse speed
till we meet Henry Ford
living on Capital Drive

let's take Obama with us
let's drive in reverse
so much the planet
will breathe a sigh of relief

let's stay in reverse
till we precede slavery
let's dance the wild
Zulu dance that comes before royalty
let's return to the purity
we all came through

let's precede the singular joy
of single malt discovery
our mistakes teaching us
something only motion knows

quickly now my dear
so my prayers won't turn
into the vomit of regret
steady like my father
heading into departure
claiming freedom from regret
when meeting mother would be
a pleasant surprise
leaving me so proud
letting me say goodbye
as a greeting

Beyond Waiting

Directly across from the hospital
a white haired lady positioned
in a large window
never moving her head
never even closing her mouth

my vision was limited
by death I guess
and another person seeing her
told me she must be awaiting her time

awaiting her time
then I could see her eyes
the only part of her that moved
I looked more closely
her eyes so blue
a blue fire in her
so I placed my hand over my heart
and bowed to her

she being released
from time saying goodbye
watching people drama
hospital traffic emergency
knowing our beauty surfaces
carries us through emptiness

Photography

Charlie gathered up his camera
hoping to photograph the sunset
so full of color near impossible
to duplicate

we stood on the dock
as the reflection increased
by the blue of the lake
two sources of light
one from the sky
turning into the mirror
of the lake

the western shore
so perfectly matching
the upside down forest
as the roots twist
into fading solar flares
trees, clouds, sky, lake
Charlie and I became part
of the reflection
our eyes became the blue
of the northern geranium
we entered strange places
that cameras only imitate

Boardwalk

For Noni and Charles

Really a spring day
black birds, red winged ones,
already returned and a neighbour
plans to shoot a goose this spring

Black birds and geese too, damn geese
coming soon, God knows I hate them
one corner of the field over there
him pointing, where they gather
always full of weeds,
good to eat though
wrap it up in strips of bacon
breast meat only, he says
and it's delicious
not too greasy??? No
not if you do it with bacon
and only the breast meat

attempted to walk the boardwalk
a thousand feet long
across the frozen swamp
arriving at the lake
had to follow the dog trail
a ridge, really a snow ridge,
very steep where I kept slipping
my foot would slide would sink
a foot or more into the snow
almost every stride
so I cut my hike short
to come back to this poem

this is a leap year
and spring is given as a gift
from the calendar designers
yet it's true, within four weeks
after Feb 29 spring makes itself known
to everyone every time
every four years
that extra day in the year
makes a beautiful spring
I know you guys will feel it
right down there in New York City

Homestead

You had to go half a mile
down an old sleigh road
the mossy trail was shadowed
with little bush flowers
squandered in places
by devil's club

giant cedar, fir and spruce
stood along the path
in such profound quiet
they shared a secret
about the story
disappearing
at their feet.

one long building
had been built
with barrel-round cedar
its roofless
ridgepole busted
by a great windfall

in the centre of the ruins
columbine gathered
a delicate prayer
of long ago logging camps
when man and horse
worked side by side

Jacob's Funeral

The priest, called twice,
did not appear

Myrtle performed
along with Tomas

she doing the ceremony
and "Father" Tomas assisting

Jacob lay quietly
in the flannelette casket

the lovely little church
swelled and the Hand Drummers

returned us to the basic, the eternal
journey of all the spirits

Myrtle conducted
Peace is flowing like a river

asking Jesus for his body
she presented the Eucharist

some went to the altar
receiving the body

I read a poem
how Jacob became the sun

we could watch him settling
through the smoke

setting like a giant star
in the forest

setting for us blessed
forever in our hearts

his power setting in the ocean
setting in the forest

ending the service
a mysterious chantress

completed the sacraments
accompanied the tolling bell

Jacob you are with us now
we are with you now

Promises

My invisible friend
where have you gone

I'm happy now
finished the dock
built a deck ladder
three steps rising
like children dreaming
of oceans can you
visualize that
can you see
the stairs I made
it gives the dock
a lot of class

with our magic
happening the town man
just gave me the angle iron
found me a piece
either two-by-two or maybe
 slightly wider
leaving me to grind the rust
then painted them black

of course I drilled first
then painted
so the dock
now is so beautiful
and I did graceful
sculpting, skill-saw
and pencil
so the arms awaiting

as you come up
from the lake
are wings

ready to take you
to the air like
an osprey
being wind-born

Sylvester the Cat

His eyes are part
of his language
and he spoke eye-talk
until I knew we were friends

once I sat beside his owner
John my brother and his eyes spoke
they said stop playing love
let's play poker

John said come here Willy
you know I love you come here
and he patted his knee
but beside John sat I

Sylvester refused to show his hand
with two games going at the same time
no said his eyes, no no no
I am sublime

his natural beauty shone
like a new star in the sky
with two golden eyes
and an ace up his sleeve

Norm Barlow

He achieved a state
of concentration
beyond anything
like meditation
for a large portion
of his time here
Norm was the
grader man

what he did was done
with care and attention
redesigning Beaver Valley Road
into a safe gravel connection
restoring that original
Roman definition
he was the
grader man

whether rich or poor
we were all indebted to him
come snow at forty below
or pothole redemption
he kept the road safe
he kept it open
he was the
grader man

a mile from the mine
was the horse logger camp
mom and dad and the kids
in a Pioneer Wall tent
all through the winter
Norm kept the road open
and he hadn't been sent
arriving with his grader
like a giant Tonka Toy
he was greeted as Royalty
by our little boy
he had time for tea
he had time for us
way back in the bush
he was the grader man

FOUR

Winter Butterfly

Adhering, upside down
to a flat rock
shielded from the weather

snowflakes thumping
against the up side
of the stone home

they, paired off,
stand in a tiny space
wings folded down

their long antennae
insulated by wing layers
of velvet insurance

dreaming all winter
of a promised
flight

Shooting the Dog

Listening to John Rutter
sing the requiem
or to Ferlingetti sing
his hydrant pissing song
will make it easier
to say that sudden
and permanent
goodbye
to Toby

he lays around
an abandoned ship
in a ship graveyard

been hanging in for a week
more or less
can hardly walk
only his own poetry
carries him up
the porch steps
his hind quarters shaking
his breath redefining labour

his diligence shines
as a beacon
in the dog world

go now proudly
old friend
go find Adrianna
and the silence
of her music

Two Bicycles

Leaning together
in the basement
like dejected defensemen
for the Boston Bruins

down the wide star-fringed road
I went swooping
by the bright windows
looking for soft green mountains
like Cape Scott
with green mist rising
singing lay my solitude down
take up a banjo
and lure me an angel
into my arms

saw a man on the corner
with a humpty-dumpty heart
so busted even angels
couldn't mend it
world so folded up
and broken
his eyes looked
like sardines
no bicycle to ride
never even skated
with the Boston Bruins

Photograph

My boy kneels
upon the pavement
wearing my tattered cap
clutching an earless teddy bear
tenderly to his heart

I have looked
at that picture so often
I can hear him laughing
a moment of recognition
causing peacefulness

peacefulness and promise
and hope as if God
had never made mistakes
as if everything would someday
be perfectly all right

as if death
had a meaning
as if life and loneliness
and separation
were part of the master plan

Revelation

This morning
three moose appeared
adrift with December snow

a large cow moose
attending two young bulls
her twins most likely
coming closer and closer
till their freedom
settled into our souls

their great bells swinging
under prehistoric heads
their interest in us
rubbing up against
our guilt

we should frighten them
we must introduce them
to people but we don't
feeling perhaps
they sensed so much more
about us than we are
ashamed of.

Tyler

May our prayer
bring you back to us
some claim you fell
through the cocaine crack

or you somehow fell
into some place rendering
invisibility
and we can not see you

the fact of instant
disappearance frightens us
someone must know something
please speak to us

among our children
you too were a child
life is so precious
a gift we can not dismiss

Cruel Kitty

Tiny mouse
soft white tummy
almost touching the floor
nose twitching in fear

he scoots across the kitchen
hides behind some cluttered toys

run, I say, get the cat
I'm thinking, she will hook it
with her terrible claws

bat it about
like a badminton bird
torture it for half an hour
leave it injured
contemplating its final destruction
                    then most likely
she will crunch the tiny bones
of its neck with her sharp teeth

run run get the cat
(cats are so cruel)

Dream Land

We were rebuilding
our old shack
making cement floors
cement walls

I had to travel
down a long country road
I met Uncle Bernard

he was on the road
not knowing where
he was heading

Uncle Bernard, Uncle Bernard
I called to him with surprise
and with questions as if I needed
him to amount to himself

he was very lonely
very sad having shrunk
having forgotten himself

I woke up then
woke to write this poem
about life wondering
if someone died

or if he belongs only to that place
where love is not made
when time keeper comes
I will visit Uncle Bernard
give him that book

the strange lady
Lillian came from this country
walked right across Canada
each footstep a century
apart looking most likely
for him

Coaxing Summer

Sandhill Cranes
singing their weird songs
while way up high in naked trees
a flock of robins
stamped against
the sky

horses come to be fed
while I stop needing
to listen
Leonard does a graceful circle
around me displaying
his gentle impatient
dance

while out into the swamp
off of the boardwalk
our sacred violinist
of silence
little Adrianna
accompanies
the giant cranes
singing through spring time
in the tall yellow
swamp grass

Whale Dream for Lorraine

We all know
way down deep
inside the gracefulness
of eternal motion
all the whales
are swimming
in the seas of heaven
shepherds exist
where once all
existence reigned
as the magic of
immortality

great creatures
were killed
chosen as necessity
overcoming basic needs
yet while we cherish
the beauty of poetry
it has always been
their strange music
that will save
our planet

the northern lights
achieve the reflection
of their songs taken
into visible syntax
connecting all of us
beyond the beyond
of forgetfulness

Mother Dream

In one of those sexy
tubular type Cadillacs
around 1956
we travelled together
across many states
me and Uncle Jim

arriving at last
on the eastern side
of Lake Dubourn
a lake renamed now to fit
more properly, they claim,
onto the tourist maps

his cabin was sliding
so slowly down the side
of Battle Point
but Uncle Jim
didn't mind

we entered on a slanted floor
painted green the wall all white
we sat on a couch adjacent
to the tiny entrance door

visitors arrived
someone named Dave
his beautiful daughter
so lovely so alive
we planned to cross the lake
to visit Mother awaiting us
both old canoeists

like when decades had passed
Part of our consciousness
included Mother
no longer just a memory
but to see her
crossing the lake
was required

the last I remember
so vividly
asking Uncle Jim
could we go to Mother soon
looking across the lake
a summer sunny day
the surface sparkling
and him telling me
we would cross soon

Moonlight for Grandma

It came sidewalking
across the lake
stopping us mid-stride
in conversation

I had climbed
the big fir
hung there
in old spurs
climbing belt
like batman
more likely
like spiderman
trembling knees
straining gut muscles
pushing towards
the big seven oh
yet achieving
one more time
the near impossible
granting entrance
to sunshine
at kitchen windows

cleaning up the cut brush
limbs and vines alike
beyond sunset
then me and my love
and her mother
shared a few moments
of perfectly balanced
light

Her Majesty

A colourful apron
of beheaded domestics
lays in crumpled repose
all along the porch

she who must remain
forever a mystery
says she refuses
that endless
flower garden
responsibility

instead and without
intention
she transforms this shack
into a magical domicile
worthy of only natural
nobility

White Rock

For Noni and Charles

Seagulls float as words
part of a script
on a page of the sky

lifting us into memories
like children left
in photographs
where dreams
are shared

everything holds here
an endless moment
of the sacred

the ocean explains
to those who have
the patience
to the rest
like us hiking along the beach
silent additions
to prayer

That Eye

For Molly

A large photograph
set directly over
my left shoulder
known in meteorological jargon
as an esoteric form
of illumination

and experience so rare
happening only on snow-
covered mountains
and my photo
revealing someone
within its radiance

the photographer
to whom I simply offer
my thanks lives surrounded
by magic

one afternoon Hayley
her brown and white dog
lay out in the field
beside me
my son had wandered off
and Hayley turned
into a shimmering white colour

while all the field around her
instantly mescaline green
then closing my eyes
crushing the vision
Hayley looked normal again

another time visiting them
two Sandhill cranes
became a center
while a large buck deer
danced around them
in perfect diameter

from the porch
we all watched, us three,
knowing beyond doubt
if only so briefly
that we were once again
within the circle
of God's eye

The Written Word

If only to see it just once
at that perfect moment
when our existence
fits perfectly
where all exist

even the invisible stars
listen at that time
even the planet realigns
even all magic rejoices
if only for that minute
when the written word
means precisely what
it means

Winter

For Tom and Donna

Their tracks
meandered side by side
like blessings
in the snow

his tracks by hers
and hers by his
it is a sight to see

on a country road
in the long moonlight
the dance it is complete

Embarking

I plan to harness Kate and Jim
an incredibly intelligent mare
and the former stallion
who still rears up
to stagger the sky
with a few statements
Mohammed Ali would copy

will hook up to two toboggans
one for me and one for memories
and head out to circle the lake

plan to enter the stillness
where islands float in the sky
and I'll sing the sad song
of Grandma's long grey hair
all the time on our journey
I'll kneel as in prayer
till my old knees remember
Latin mass holiness
and the horses
become wild
once more

Her Eye

She kept one eye open
while departing
knowing after the light
had revealed her secret
her light secret
that it was best
to look in both directions
until the light
on this side
went out

she left us
between the before
and the here after
her eye staring at us
across the wrinkles of bed linen
transformed into mountain ranges
telling us to live
in that perfect reflection
defined by her hatred
and her love

she could see us flying
and I floated around the bed
attempting to shed her
of regret
having lost her son
being abandoned
by her lover
that grief burden
regret would not appease

who is he
she asked her mother
knowing I don't exist
like her mother
or her brother

Promising

As I near my time
pushing sixty nine
can't help

wondering how
flying saucers
and serious dishes

mother used
as weapons demanding
promises we would

never not even
ever rationalize
striking brothers

or sisters
not once even
and her sixty seven

leaving with wind
so powerful it called
me from sleep

dreaming total nonsense
of religious possibilities
after years of lent

never slept in her bed
post puberty the floor
beside it

that night
was more than good enough
when she came home

a shrieking power wind
slamming shutters
more powerful

than fear
or sudden recognition
of God

nothing to be expected
like Dad prepared for
at eighty seven

with those extra years
as his angel time
beyond us then

flip the coin for me
bravery on one side
the wind on the other

Mother my love
is a son's

Motocross

Endless moments accumulating
on the very edge of awareness
like that side road mountain
where a grassy slope was covered
with small beds of purple flowers
a special place where the mountains
reveal their ceremony
of sundown

while we race by
hoping for light enough
to cook a late dinner
on the tail gate
that industrial altar
upon which our celebration
will take place

off loading bikes, the tent
cooler and cook gear
my son suddenly stops
Dad look at those fingers
created by beams of light
where a giant baby gently curls
her fingers over the peak
of the western mountain
slowly revealing us
our tent, trailers, pick-ups
the odd person quad driving
across the valley floor

of the Whispering Pine Rez
everything twilight reduced
ant size to that great giant
of light while tiny freight trains
work their way up river
just across from camp

Six Swans

The day our daughter
celebrated her birthday
ice disappeared from the lake

the very next day
March 26, six swans arrived
and they wore the lake
like a great gown
which reached back
through the renaissance
making it impossible to imagine
one of them named George
and the other Joanne

they stayed here
with the hungry eagle
making passes over them
till they decided to leave

one day we noticed their absence
and the lake noticed too
it grew very quiet
not the stillness
created by beauty
but the quiet of funerals
which slips up on you
unwanted

Sandhill Cranes Again

For a full hour
flocks of cranes came chortling
into a rendezvous place where
the sky was a neighbourhood

I counted fifteen, some four or five hundred
strong, they would join up with another
group and then begin spiraling
down into a deep twister
faster and faster
and from my vantage point
they moved so fast
they changed
shreds of some ancient language
a spiral of words
a mandala
a corkscrew twisting
where power awaits them
and just as sudden
as they first appeared
they form that happy V
for peace brother
and haul ass for warmer places
leaving me feeling like part
of the wind

Slow Motion

Today the snowflakes
are so large
so slow and so lazy
barges drifting by
clinging to the clouds

they do not wish to fall
swinging back and forth
in their slow-motion dance
from some exotic tropic island

sometimes they swing up
then they swing down
till gently they touch
the ground

Barkerville

Three long exceeding
thin fingers extended
as if surrealists
had painted them

eagerness beyond
explanation reaching
into wide flaring nostril

one permanent wheelchair
resident large head and neck
braced chemical supplication
constant his hollywood
whiskered face

forehead twisted and broad
skull pushed into birth
presence suddenly revealed

baby laughter attuned
to deep baritone chords
greets our gigantic
stagecoach horses

he repeats these few notes
two or three times
he can't restrain himself

among hundreds of people
his nurse wheels him in
up the street his laughter
a blessing trailing
in the wind

Raven Small

I live on the mountain
it is a holy place
and I know the black raven
I know his purple sound

I seen him transformed
like my curses on the mountain
I seen once how the coal-black
of his feathers turned luminous silver blue
just like my curses
they turn into praises
in that special place

nobody else truly understands
how it is that I could not change
while in that place everything
was changed around me

nobody really understood
and it didn't matter
the Raven knows
he changes the curses for me
but for everyone else
they are just profane
in a holy place
and not prayers at all
just me being small

Transformations

After a life time
or two life times
working with horses
it becomes easy to drift
into places we usually avoid
like places where different animals
transform into fish or birds
just for the moment
when we have moments
days that are not paid for

driving the gentle giants
after skidding giant logs for a day
or half a day or a day and a half a day
and every ounce of ton working quietly
so the Clydesdales pull homeward
like a gift for the king of exclamation marks
ee cummings all mixed into legendary
        dream places

just as we turn into our driveway
three young and very fast quarterhorses
meet us all excited and begin
darting to and fro across our path
like darning with high speed needles
jibing the giants around turning them
into two great whales greeted by dolphins
making me a small part of their joyful
moments beyond definition of any sort
Linda's lovely mares just a treat
for my old eyes and my big friends
take me home mama take me home again

New Glasses

Announcing Hamish
into a painting of Granville
that restaurant in Quesnel linking
all restaurants achieving
restaurant identity

visiting together
called breakfast
discovering the small god
of eternal innocence
smiling at us,
for us, with us,
blessing with his purity
with his presence
knowing everything
his mother smiling
leaving saying
bye bye bye
so he smiles again
for us which he does
for us
leaving us his space
before teeth even

later at Walmart
two young men brandishing
small baseball bats
head for the cashier
with lovers following
I'm wishing
with my new glasses
the glasses that leave out nothing

wish they would grant me courage
enough to tell them
to reconsider
to take the other path
forever and forever
never forget
the announcement
of Hamish

Wolves Return

Beyond the latitude
of northern lights
held torch like
solar power
celebrates

the wolves return
neither intended
nor imagined
but to sing release
with grief

thinking Howard died today
I take my silver flute
and call out two long notes
to those wild brothers of mine
alpha delta phi
scattered like stars across the sky
I need you now
more than ever
even more
than before

the wolves have gone
as players claim
they've moved on
though the response
comes from our Clydesdale
Lady bulging through
flaring nostrils
thundering around
in our corral

FIVE

Beyond Doubt

My body has become
a personal type of disgust
after seven decades of delight
I now find it repulsive

perhaps this is the first
realization preparing me
for departure

yet what shreds of soul
still singing to me
cause doubt beyond despair

doubt is far more positive
than I was taught
to expect

like at long last
one leg shorter than the other
feet arched almost into mythology
and a penis that hangs
like an old prayer
in a burnt out church
rolls of fat surrounding me
yet her name appears unexpectedly

many times I wanted
to phone her
ask her anything
just listen to her voice
as she calls my name

do our names belong
together when only
doubt remains
do I have enough courage
to walk alone
to sing sad songs
remembering every time
every dream
expecting to disappear
while I am still here

no wonder my friends
chastise me claiming
you are no longer
that one-lady man
as if that was
a kind of consolation
when one woman alone
no longer loves me

yet, just, perhaps
she does
in spite of my old body
my old dreams
love is no longer enough
I need so much more
to even like myself

Jet Vision

As we level out
forty thousand feet up
our vision covers
an easy hundred miles
or more

it's the big rivers
that continue
to frighten me

are those large ones
associated with tar sands
or are they still free?

in Alberta large rivers
come down from the north
destroying Native communities
poisoning fish and moose
and people

don't the people
in the south
properly understand
gravity

A Valentine

Recently finished barn
its roof carefully built
covered with galvanized metal
reflecting its shape
up into the stars

the wide blade of Old Granny
1956 D6 Cat, 9-U heritage
gently swinging to remove banks of snow
heaped up below the roof edge
the upper corner of the Granny canopy
caught the corner of the barn's roof
twisting two-by-fours into splinters
mangling the barn's silver skin

you broke into tears
at that demolition
repairs took most of a day;
two-by-fours carefully cut back
inventive angles sculpted
to reassemble the corner
the mangled roofing removed
and three short pieces inserted
ending up with a corner more powerful
than the original

the square of the corner
a poem to the barn
it gives it something
the original had lacked
a simple attempt to celebrate
square constellations,

that small square
reestablishes the barn into
imagination, it will always
take me back into your arms
a small part of the religion
of log barn redemption

My Love

I sit in the van
when she shops
in the large
grocery store

cars, trucks
pedestrians constantly
making endless traffic

my poem
keeps me company

a diesel pick-up
rattles into ignition
some lady at the wheel

on this side
of our round planet
silence is almost forbidden

demanding a dance
of commotion
we create smoke

it rises
along with slams
shouts and moments
hurried and lonely

Connection

for Diana

That's what it was:
you bending down
to the horse's feet
silver file shedding
flakes of white memories
then you and the giant
suddenly clouded;
tiny blizzard
ice crystals breeze blown
sun gift from great pine
a kind of baptism

beautiful strands
of white claiming
permanence
within the golden cascade
of your hair
holding the image
sacred and clear
sudden definition:
deep within us
the bell tolling
a singular true note

Pioneer Logging Tape

My daughter misplaced it
the logging tape, complete
with the little logger depicted
bucking the butt end off a big log
wearing an American Hardhat,
aluminum most likely, feeding out tape
measuring something mysterious

most likely left the tape
in the snow beside her last skid
which I had pushed onto the deck
with our old D6 Cat

finally I asked St. Anthony
get off your saintly ass Antoine
and help me find this tape
next day delimbing a big pine
I was suddenly startled:
someone standing beside me
dark hair, raven black and blue shirt
ocean blue, that blue midsummer afternoon
drifting further and further in a rolling
fish boat the sun revealing a blue shade
so deep and mysterious
that was the color of his shirt
slight beard and short hair
his expression so calm, so peaceful,
so welcome he appeared from
light years of intensity

then disappeared in a true second;
a free-fall second, a first
when arms are winding windmills
hands desperate at pulling the rip cord
he was gone that fast and had I not turned
to look again where he had been standing
part ways between hope and doubt
I would not have seen the yellow ribbon
of the tape, inches on one side,
metric on the other, partially buried
in the brush and snow pushed up by the deck

Post Brain Surgery

Dad, says the youngster
with question marks floating
like invisible spirits all
caught up in the tone
of his undulations

were you always
retarded I mean
the way you talk
to the cat for instance
you never did that before
and even your thoughts

they crash up against
the shoreline and you
never even got out
onto the lake yet

Broken Glasses

Lady of love
and of hopelessness
how I miss your morning breath
on my morning neck

ah woman
so miserable of mornings
how miserable empty
this emptiness

I'd have your fierce anger
even your distress
oh lady of lilacs
and heartlessness

lady of doubt
and flowers and miracles
listen close
while the light
is still fresh

the wind blows
the sun bugles
this morning

sings in motion
seagulls swear
in seagull slang

dogs bark for everything
hand holding moments
of spring

the fuller day awaits us
with no promises oh beautiful lady
of righteousness

your pride crushes too much
your silence sounds as frozen birds
breaking into cubes of green ice

your confusion and mine
meet somewhere alone
two drunken philosophers

arguing first causes
and the great way
smashing empty glasses

all their fine talk
surrounding them
with broken glass

let us leave them
to bury themselves
while our hearts

still surrounded
with flowers come home again
as clear as mauve starlight

Connecting

For months I studied
places where you might appear
as if you were almost invisible
like the lynx who often hunts
during the daytime
when the dogs hounded him
tearing up that spruce
then leaping to a smaller tree
settling like a dream
onto one of its limbs
forty feet in the sky
and perfectly parallel
to old Earth

the lynx pulled everything together
ground, sky, tree, cloud
sunlight and darkness until
the hunting adventure
almost forgotten
the dogs, restless, eager
to chase rabbits
a notion likely suggested
by the lynx as he became
part of the tree

once glancing onto the contour
of that ridge we drive by so often
just once and only in a glance
its beautiful body lay there
a hundred feet from the road
then last night representing
the twenty first century

moving at seventy clicks
I found it by surprise
hunched over a rabbit
it had caught
and incredibly graceful
shifting your shoulders
you swung your upper body
directly toward the bright eyes
of monster car
with me wondering if you know
that me, a human, was behind
the glass or that you even cared

now I look for you again
hiding down among the keys
of this deluxe typewriter
which somehow takes me to John
when you that time drowned
how it was your body found
right where I knew it was
how come all that grace
holds me to you John

the cougar and John
must be a connection
conjured by the power
just before sunrise
as I write this poem
while it becomes something
cougars, rabbits, night time,
memory, enemies and friends

all connected up in poems
like the lynx and the dogs
the tree and the clouds
and you John so great
finding you again

Presentation

As we grow older
my true love said
fat grows upon us
not in bulges or pillows
but in wrinkles instead

you remind me, she said,
of that little Charpai
that your brother loves
a little sad fellow from China
whose face is cramped with wrinkles

with me, she confided,
it just pulls away
no patterns, no wrinkles
just sort of a filling
settling where it might

only more to love
is what I always knew
not that wrinkles
offered my inner beauty
but that fat itself
only became musical

not the finest violin
on this planet compares
nor the highest mountain
the deepest moment
of hesitation
nothing compares
with what is so
profoundly present

My Woman's Gone Away

It's one of those Jacob nights
when I could use me an angel
to wrestle with til dawn
my bed is cold and unfriendly
since my woman went to town

the radio
my only companion
hip station went
and found Jesus
while we were loving
in the hay-ricking sun
all that fire
in our passion
but now I'm alone

I see me limping
to my grave
the sun a faint kiss
on my shoulder
my heart full
of gratitude
my ragged pockets
filled with bright promises
your soft kisses sprinkled
all over my face

Jesus is kept
in a drifting smoke-ring
since resurrection
protected in a fragile dream
where no mean person

can find him
make him bleed
again

now when I come
to the dancing hill
and they ask me
as they surely will
if I been singing and saving
I'll admit I spent my love
in this poet's passion
I'll tell the fisherman
about your smile
demanding poetic
attention

I'll present arguments
larger than loneliness
confess a desire
for salvation
however true
this may become
the entire redemption
against my misery now
compares nothing

Love Gift

For Audrey Geensen

Holy gratitude
Adrianna the princess
ordering the King,
her father,
at odd hours
as she lay
in hospital bed
downtown for restaurant treats
only a real princess could imagine

she gave us everything
including anger, frustration
and the need to blame
shouting out she saw the light
revealing a love so deep
it shone through our doubt
leaving us all of our short
comings, big trees
we could cling to
when that terrible wind
tore her away from us

Ladder

May 96

Just dying would have been adequate
normally there is some sort of trace
a connection greater than memory

beyond the usual litany:
grief, sorrow, regret, guilt
I'd hoped for a sense
of continual presence:
an empty chair
full of emptiness
an extra place-setting
something beyond bone-trust
vanishing to dust

once when we were driving
I discovered a tiny line on your face
a crinkle where your lip curved

me talking, looking over
seeing a line that blossomed
into an understanding

it's unfair that this is what I cling to
that one line on your face
like a rung on a ladder

the ladder is floating
above the story sea
above the windy trees

the stars reversing
forever
you left, otherwise,
without a trace as they say
abiding patiently, courageously
in your deep blood nature

you insisted on unrequired expectations
as if you could control the exit
and you did as a parting gesture
of paternal pride

and I don't need anything more
yet I have the ladder
which I won't let slip,
just a rung really

Domestic Thing Again

And have I not wound
my fingers in yellow clouds
when she lay in my bed

her hair whispered
the seret name of my hands
when we were lovers

dancing on the air I heard
angels laughing somewhere
and the sweet voice of a flute climbing
up through the blue branches
of the clouds

oh how we carry on
in this long tradition
of spring

ask the little mouse
who stumbled in during
a dark argument, probably has
an idea or two of his own

his minuscule electric-wire tail
connecting him to the big outside world
no wonder he fled back through the hole
in the baseboard no bigger'n a thimble
when you cried a real tear

bet he figured he
would be electrocuted
all that energy falling
into one huge silver puddle

Post Percutaneous C.I.

March 04

Not holding back
just slowly walking
sitting in the Sassafras
conversation sounds rising
sudden laughter
a flock of snow birds

people walking by
every race, size, shape
yet modest costume
strolling blessings

everything enjoyed
beyond expectation
some physically
hand connected

Prairie Ocean

For Adam

Heading out across
this big ocean prairie
cattle studded on the
lumpy sea of it

and the morning light
like mescaline on the snow
and I'm thinking about you Adam

a lady told me to forget you
leave the boy behind
in the smoke of your heart
and start another family

as if families just get started
and its a big sky here Adam
one day you will be coming
out here over this prairie
maybe looking for a horse
like I'm doing

keeping eyes eagle edged
for the spooky antelope
and the coyote all alone
maybe see that grove
of willow with all
the crows nests in it

keeping an eye
on the far blue ridge
like looking at the horizon
of yesterday

I feel your little hand
coming into mine like a prayer
as we cross the street
and the big stringy prairie
waist deep in buffalo bones
and the silence of Indians
following great silver herds
across lost sleeping dreams

we all come down
to loss inside us
before we know
there is no other way
to look but through
the eyes of our hearts

and you be thinking that
coming into the foothills
with the same clouds
smeared against the blue canvas sky
and you won't be forgetting
your own father either

the holy emptiness
of this big place
holds you warm
in my heart little man
your heart be

as big and as free
as the prairie
with the gas station on it
and to me everything here
is just as it is
like you coming up behind me
throwing your little arms
around my neck

I ain't looking back
through the smoke
of my life because
I like looking back
but sometimes
when you look
through the smoke
it makes your eyes water
and the water cleans your eyes
and after a while
you see everything
by the simple name of it

Rocky Mountain Ash

For Adam

They say the red
berries will kill
but I am not so sure

it's true they are bitter
and I know their colour
is too bright
too pure

but when you danced
under that tree today
teasing me pretending
to eat its fruit

I was frightened
for a moment
until you, you natural magician,
you began spitting out the stones
which turned into tiny silver bells
as they fell into the palm
of your father's hand

Later

He had opened up
one side of my skull
gently folding back
part of my brain
away from the aneurysm
he worked on me
inside my skull
for hours and hours
it seemed
nowhere for me
an empty place

later perhaps days later
I recognized him
the gentle healer
with a name like
brown leaf as if
he belonged to something
beyond vocabulary
and his name was Brownlee
Doctor Richard Brownlee

he was enshrouded
by a golden aura
not one letter
of exaggeration
a golden aura
him and one of the nurses
for weeks I saw them
without words
whatsoever
in that healing place
from which I was
slowly emerging

one day I asked my love
can you see the aura

a crimson electric color
after that I saw only sparks
of the aura around him

I began returning
to this side
of mystery

then only imagined
that which I had seen

imagined how the doctor
emerged from
pure light